# CREATIVE WRITING COURSE

This book's ideas are derived from the author's years of research and compilation. Any similarity to other people's books is coincidental and not intentional.

No part of this publication may be reproduced, stored in a retrieval system, or transmitted in any form or by any means, electronic, mechanical, digital, photocopy, recording, or otherwise - except for brief quotations in printed reviews - without the prior, written permission of the copyright owner.

ISBN: 979-8-9917974-6-7

Copyright 2025 by Susan M. Magras-Edwards

Written by Susan Magras-Edwards

Book design and layout by Susan M. Magras-Edwards/Magras Literary Entertainment MLE (www.magrasliterary.com)

Published by Magras Literary Entertainment

Front and Back Cover Design Adapted from Canva

Printed in the USA

# Getting To Know The Author

Susan M. Edwards is a wife, mother, former educator, avid reader, writer, pet lover, and entrepreneur. She was born and raised on the island of St. Thomas, United States Virgin Islands. She now resides in sunny Southern California. She has two grown children, two daughters-in-law, two grandsons, and a vast extended family.

Susan spent many years working in the accounting field. Eventually, she became a teacher and worked for 17+ years. While she enjoyed teaching, she decided there were other ways she could teach and express her creativity and imagination without doing so in a classroom setting.

Through the years, Susan worked with many high school and college students, proofreading and editing their documents. She earned a bachelor's degree in business administration, a master's in organizational management (Human Resources), and a master's in education (Elementary Education).

Susan finally decided to publish her first book in 2019. Eventually, despite some setbacks, her book was first published in 2020, and printed copies became available in 2021. Her journey in writing continues with this and several other books, a cookbook, and multiple puzzle books.

# TABLE OF CONTENTS

- Acknowledgments
- Introduction
- What is Creativity
    - Boosting Creativity
    - Creativity Trigger
- Drop the Self-criticism
- Be Positive
- The Building Process
- Changing Your Environment
- Three Things You Need to Know Before You Start Writing
    - Creating Characters
    - Creating Your Story's Setting
    - Capitalizing On an Image or Event
- The "Don't" of Creative Writing
- The Nuts and Bolts of Creative Writing
    - Brainstorming
    - Keeping a Journal
    - Training Yourself to Describe The World Around You
    - Staying Focused
    - What Do You Like to Write?
    - What Is Your Direction?
- Your Emotional Connection to Your Writing
    - Real Imagining
- Poetry
- What is Science Fiction
    - Five Tips for Writing a Science Fiction Novel
- Writing Adventure Stories
- Tips to Help You Write Your Best Adventure Story Yet
    - Read Popular Novels
    - Structure Your Story With a Basic Adventure Framework
    - Create a Compelling Main Character

- 
    - Introduce a Catalyst
    - Develop Strong Supporting Characters
    - Create or Find a Setting That Takes Your Story to the Next Level, Elevating the Risks
    - Pace Your Story Correctly
    - Increase the Risks Your Characters Take Throughout the Story
    - Set a Deadline for Your Antagonist
    - Allow Your Protagonist to Transform Throughout the Story
- Writing Suspenseful Thrillers – Tips for Writing Mystery Stories
- How to Write a Romance
    - Writing Tips for Romance Novels
    - Creating Intimate Scenes
    - Developing Supporting Characters
    - Does Your Romance Novel Have the Potential to Become a Series
    - Writing Happy Endings
- Writing Drama-Filled Stories
- Nailing Your Dialogue
- Use of Metaphors
- Writing an Autobiography
- Point of View
- Plot, Structure, and Narratives
    - What is the Plot, Anyway?
    - Structure: The Glue That Holds It All Together
    - Narratives
- Making Tough Decisions
    - Reaching the Finish Line
    - Revising: Making Necessary Changes
- Your Book is Finished: What Now?
    - Outside Reviews
    - Listening to Constructive Criticism
    - A Dynamic Finish: The Final Run
    - Agents: Should You Get One, and Why?
    - On to the Follow-up

- o Reading Critics
- Conclusion
- References
- Other Books By This Author

# Acknowledgments

I want to thank God for the inspiration, talent, and skills He has blessed me with so I could write this book. I want to thank my family, extended family, and friends who have supported me through the years and encouraged my passion for writing. I am incredibly grateful and appreciate all of you so much!

Your decision to purchase and read my book is more than a transaction. It is a validation of my work and a testament to the power of storytelling. Writing is a part of who I am, and your support has been a driving force in my life journey. I have been inspired by the children I worked with for over 17 years, and your readership has further fueled my passion for storytelling. Your interest in my work and your feedback have been invaluable. I hope my stories inspire you to do your best, strive for success, and remember that it is not where you start but where you finish. Your support has made this book possible and inspired me to continue writing and sharing my stories because I believe in the transformative power of storytelling.

Susan M. Magras-Edwards

# Introduction

I have found that good writing comes from constantly practicing repeatedly. Like anything else we want to become proficient in, it requires effort and long-term commitment. If you're going to become a great writer, you must begin writing. I have had plenty of practice over the years, yet I continually strive to perfect my art. Whether writing for myself or others, I strive for excellence in writing.

As writers, we often worry about whether people will love our writing. We spend so much wasted time thinking about other people's opinions that we postpone following our dream of becoming writers or giving up on our dream entirely. The best way to become the writer you envision is to sit down with a pen and paper and start jotting down ideas or whatever comes to your mind. My favorite thing to do is write in my journal, and I have many journals sitting on my bookshelves with ideas and thoughts that I look back on and review for my subsequent written work.

I aim to teach you how to stir your creative juices in this course. I would also like you to learn the various methods and techniques I have used to help me progress with my writing. People have said that teaching creativity is impossible; however, I believe it is. Over the years, many individuals have told me they could be more talented, knowledgeable, experienced, or skilled enough to become a great writer. Yes, you are. It will take learning new skills and a commitment, but you can learn to bring forth the creativity you have hidden within you to become a better writer with time and practice.

There is no one-size-fits-all solution to the writing challenges we each face, and of course, I cannot guarantee anything through this course. However, I will do my best to help you improve your writing skills so you can create your unique writing success. By becoming a better and more creative writer, you can enhance your list of life skills and express yourself through the written word more easily.

When I write, I enter my world, and my imagination starts to run free, allowing me to write whatever comes to my mind. I try not to worry about what others will think or say, and I push back at the fear that tries to creep into my mind. I allow myself a chance to write freely, uncensored by the outside world. Before long, I find I have written plenty of words, and my creativity smiles at me from the pages I have written. I hope you, too, will see your potential at the end of this course and experience the birth of your creativity on the pages you write.

## What is Creativity?

Creativity is the ability, an attitude, and a process. Creativity is the ability to imagine or invent something new. We all can do this, yet many of us hide this ability for many reasons. Sometimes, it's because of fear; other times, it's because we don't want to be judged by others, or perhaps we have suppressed it for so long, shuffling along in life, that we forget it is in us. Whatever the reason is, isn't it time to dig it out, dust it off, and breathe life into it once again?

Creativity is an attitude. It's our ability to accept change, new things, new ideas and the willingness to embrace the possibilities right before us. It's the mixing together of things that might not traditionally go together. I, for example, love banana sandwiches. Some people may think that sounds weird, but to me, it's when other people make sandwiches that include bananas and pickles or put ketchup on their eggs. Not that there is anything wrong with those things; I would not personally do that myself. People come up with crazy ideas all of the time, and while it might be unbelievable to you or me, it might seem perfectly normal to them.

Creativity is also a process. Creative people are always working hard to create or improve ideas. They are always coming up with unique solutions to a variety of problems or situations that arise. One thing I have found is that creativity only happens sometimes. It occurs after much thought and consideration. Think about some idea or solution you have come up with. It could be related to writing, or it could be something from your job, but wherever the idea came from, once you got the picture in your head, you had to go through a process in your mind, perhaps even through trial and error, to determine if it would work. Believe it or not, this is what happens with most ideas. So you might ask yourself, especially if creativity does not feel natural, how can I boost my creativity? How can I bring out those long-dormant ideas in the recesses of my mind?

## *Boosting Creativity*

Before I go to the course's nitty-gritty, I would like to provide some tips that may help you boost your creativity. First, you should commit yourself to creativity in general. What do I mean by that? Well, you should begin by telling yourself that you can be creative. Positive thoughts and vibes help me when I am at a loss for words to write, and once our mind starts thinking positively about what we desire, it opens us up to speaking and writing freely. Next, you should want to become a master at your craft. It means practicing writing, much like an athlete practices their craft until they are considered experts in their field. Third, reward your curiosity. If you are interested in learning something new, check it out.

Do your research and investigate the possibilities. Then, take risks. When we hear the word risk, we often think of negative thoughts. However, if we are never willing to take risks in life, we may never know our true potential. Go for it!

Build your confidence by practicing your craft. Find a trusted person who will give you honest feedback without putting you down. In time, you will build your confidence and be willing to take your writing to the next level. Make time to write. Walk around with a notebook or journal and note whatever comes to mind at every opportunity. Overcome a negative attitude about yourself and your writing. If we walk around thinking and acting negatively, we are bound not to follow our dream of becoming better writers. I have had to overcome fear and negative feelings about myself and my writing to see my first book become a published work. Fear of failure or rejection often keeps us from moving ahead, which is something most of us experience at one time or another. We must fight these feelings so we can become better at our craft.

One thing you can do is collaborate with others. Work with others who want to write a genre similar to yours. Participate in writers' workshops or get together with others to form a book club. Find inspiration from others in the industry. You can join social media groups with writers to learn what they are doing to keep things fresh and new. One of my favorite tips is to unplug or unwind and do nothing. If an idea hits me, I keep my journal or notebook nearby, but clearing my mind gets my creative juices flowing. Another tip is to walk, particularly if you have hit a wall in your writing. I take my headphones, turn on some music, and walk to clear my head. It does not have to be a lengthy walk. Thirty minutes is a good number, and you will get some exercise.

I don't necessarily use this tip, but others have used the Six Thinking Hats Technique to boost creativity. **The Six Thinking Hats** is a role-playing model by Edward de Bono in 1986. (You can find his book on Amazon and other book sites if you desire to learn more about his techniques.) It is a team-based problem-solving and brainstorming technique to explore problems and solutions to uncover ideas and options that a homogeneous thinking group might otherwise overlook. I find this helpful when you are in a job setting and collaborating with a team to produce new and creative ideas to boost sales or marketing. I am sure other writers probably use this technique, but I have not used it for that purpose and cannot speak to it here in this context. It is merely a suggestion on my part to help you with your creativity.

One tip I do use with frequency is to set the right mood. If my mood is off, I cannot write, and writer's block will set in. This may require me to put on some soft music in the background. Other times, I may need a quiet place with no distractions. I close my office door and focus on what I want to write to accomplish my goals. If I am at a loss, I may ask for advice or get feedback from a close friend, one of my children, or my husband. It always helps when I explain what I am trying to say when I reach out for help. They may have an alternative way to say something I have not thought of and open my mind to other opinions.

As time has passed, I have improved at observing my surroundings and paying attention to details. Being detail-oriented is not just for people looking for a job; it is vital to becoming a better writer. Paying attention to details in your surroundings, how people converse, descriptive words and phrases, trends, and more can open your mind to being more descriptive and detailed in your writing.

Are you one of those who consistently make excuses that you are too busy? I was one of those people, but I have learned that I must un-busy myself to write and follow my passion. Slow down your pace, and do not rush yourself. As I have said before, make time to write. Find what gets you excited about writing. When you think about it, that person or thing becomes the catalyst that drives your writing. Do not focus on too many things all at once. Focus on one thing at a time and write about that. Pick a topic and write down everything you know about it. Before long, you will have a page or two or perhaps more on that topic.

Before we move forward, let me say there are five main ingredients to getting your creativity moving in the right direction. They are finding alone time, building curiosity and exploration, taking risks and working hard, accepting mistakes and the need to start over, and believing in yourself and that you can and will open up and find the creativity in your writing that seems missing on occasion.

## *Creativity Triggers*

When I am out and about, I am always looking and listening for creative triggers that may help me when writing. These might be a chance remark by someone, a problem presented, a solution found, or deliberate thoughts that pop into my mind that I stew on to see if they will trigger any ideas. I pay attention to my surroundings. I write descriptions of scenes that I may use later when writing a story. I work on thinking creatively, often using one or more of the five creative methods that make up the creative process. I believe we all have creativity within us and never really lose it. However, I think there are times when we have too much going on, and we lose touch with it or lose our belief in ourselves and our creative abilities. Creative thinking comprises three key elements: absorption, reflection, and inspiration. We absorb information and details, reflect on what we learned, and use this information to inspire us toward new ideas. There are four major components to the creative process. Every creative process goes through these four states: preparation, incubation, illumination, and verification. I find that where my creative process begins depends partly on whether I have any ideas about what I will write. I am not a scientist, and I will not pretend to be one, but I believe that we all go through this creative process, whether for writing, crafting a work or school assignment, or some other task that requires us to come up with a new idea.

## *Drop the Self-criticism*

Ideally, if you want to get your creative juicing flowing, stop criticizing yourself. Self-criticism will often block your creative juices from flowing and limit new ideas. You must recognize when doing this to yourself and learn to control it quickly. When you are in a self-criticizing mood, it is difficult to recognize the difference between good and bad ideas. To acknowledge that even when an idea seems terrible, it can later be cleaned up and polished into a shiny new idea that can work for a different writing project than the one you are currently on. Be patient with yourself and recognize that creativity is a process that takes time and practice.

I find that reading stimulates my brain. I love reading, and I always tell my students that reading allows me to travel to places I have never been to or have dreamed about visiting.

Reading opens up possibilities and inspires me to increase my creativity. When I read the types of genres I love writing, I have found that it helps me learn techniques and strategies. If that does not help increase your creativity, find something you love to read and notice how the author shares their creativity through descriptive words, scenes, or narrative. By reading materials that stimulate my creativity, I can get past negative thinking and move towards creative thinking.

Practice daily toward improving your writing. Write about something new every day. Can't write every day? Write as often as you can and make time to learn about new things. Understand and accept that there is always room for improvement in your writing. Explore new opportunities as they will give you a fresh perspective on your writing. I get inspired when I read or hear about something new and different. I am always open to learning new things and challenge myself to look at things objectively and openly to keep things moving. All these things and more can get you out of a negative funk and on a creative trend.

## *Be Positive*

With everything happening in our world today, it is easy for us to become wrapped up in the negativity that seems to emanate from every aspect of our lives. Make it a habit to push those negative thoughts out of your mind. Research has shown that when we have a positive outlook on life, it encourages and enhances our creative thinking. When I feel positive, my writing shows my willingness to be more daring and explore new and adventurous things. I am much more flexible, which opens my mind to more creative thinking. I try my hardest not to allow my disappointments and mistakes in writing to take away my feelings of inspiration, creative ideas, and drive to dig deep and come up with some of my best-written work.

## *The Building Process*

When all else fails, and I am not in a creative mood, I pull out one of those 1000-piece puzzles my younger son gave us for Christmas one year. I begin putting it together, and figuring out which piece goes where helps me regain the feeling that I am building something. I love using my hands to make things, and when I am crafting, sewing, or creating wood projects, this time helps me get very creative, even when I started with my thoughts being disjointed and out of sorts. In the same way, our body needs nourishment, and so does our creativity. If your mind is bogged down constantly with the hustle and bustle of life, your creativity will likely slow instead of flourishing as it should. Creativity is not about having everything at our fingertips when we need it but the ability to create something out of nothing that can be of use later. Thus, the notebooks and journals I mentioned before. I am a visual learner, and 65% of the population is visual learners. To help with my writing, I will use pictures or drawings to help visualize a scene or characters I am developing. Keep in mind that you do not need to be a great artist. I would often tell my students to start with stick people. I realize that may sound funny, but it works, and I am willing to use whatever works so long as it works.

## *Changing Your Environment*

A change in scenery is often the key to getting your creativity flowing. If you are like me and often on a fixed budget, an out-of-town trip might not be in the cards, but a trip to a local park might be the ticket you need to get your creative thoughts flowing again. If you live near a beach or lake, those too may be an option to unlock the creative block in your mind. In the past, I would redecorate a room in my house; most recently, I rearranged my office/workspace. These would help me clear my mind, plus the clutter that was building up in my space. When there is too much clutter or chaos around me, my mind tends to wander, and I cannot focus on the writing task. I free up my space to gain a new perspective on my living environment. Watch a decorating show or visit a showroom or model home. Do something different to change the scene around you. It may help to free up your mind and allow your creative process to flow.

# Three Things You Need to Know Before You Start Writing

There are three things you should know before you start writing. First, you should have some idea about what you want to write. You do not need to know everything before writing, but you should know your novel's topic or plot. Usually, before I write, I jot down ideas for my writing piece. I try to grasp what I want to say or what I want my story to be. I often glean ideas from my surroundings or previously written notes in journals or notebooks. I ensure I have spent time thinking about, studying, or researching my topic.

## *Creating Characters*

When I wrote my first book, I got inspiration from the little pictures of cupcakes with students' names on a teacher's wall. I started drawing cupcakes with legs and arms and formulated characters in my mind. I sat down and drew out my primary story characters and a couple of preliminary chapters for the story in a few short days. From there on, the story developed into the book I have today. Knowing and understanding the main character of your storyline is essential, as that character will determine the direction you take when writing. I realize we have great technology, but I am not always at my computer. With that in mind, I walk with a notebook in my purse or car. I took my notebook in my teacher tool bag when working as a teacher. As I gather ideas for supporting characters or the antagonists in my story, I jot those down in my notebook. Your characters should be speaking to you so you can write down details about them. You have to interview them if they are not talking to you. Wait, what? Ask them questions in your head like you were asking a friend for detailed information about them.

Here are some examples of questions you might ask your characters to answer:
- What do you value most in life?
- What do you want?
- What color is your hair?
- Tell me about yourself.
- What do you like to do?
- What are some things you need?
- Who are your friends?
- What inspires you?
- What are some things you do not like?

## Creating Your Story's Setting

Since some of my writing is adventure/mystery stories, I need to know what the primary setting looks like so that even if I don't describe it in every detail, I still know how it looks and feels. I am detail-oriented in these books and love to describe the scenery, sounds, and feelings I would get if I were in person. I place myself into each scene and envision what I see, feel, and hear. As a writer, I must deeply understand my setting as it allows me to feel confident and free to write more details. In my mind, I can interact with the setting as I would the characters, and it makes for more descriptive wording. I want my readers to visualize and feel as though they are experiencing what the characters are within the story. I will often use settings I already know, such as my hometown, workplace, a place I have visited, or a school setting. For you, it might be a favorite restaurant, beach, park, or other frequented area.

## *Capitalizing On An Image Or Event*

When planning to write a story, I often visualize what or where I would love my characters to go. I may conjure up an image or some significant event that will be the key to my story; my first book was Cupcake Island, a fictional place I only had a name for initially. I also created a name for my organization, which I changed three times before coming up with the one I chose in the book. I also wanted the team to travel to them and their organization on a unique flying ship. I knew the main plot idea but had no idea where it would go and how I would take my story from beginning to end. Having the various images in my head and eventually on paper allowed me to be creative with my content and expand on my ideas to engage my readers and capture their imaginations with words and descriptions of each scene throughout the story.

## The "Don't" of Creative Writing

Only try to teach a lesson after you write the story. It is very tempting, but don't do it! The moral of a story should not dictate it but enhance it instead. Your job as a writer is to tell a story. Facts tell, but stories sell. You must remember that, particularly if you plan to write for a living. You want your storyline to be full of life, so understand that if you try to tell a story to teach a moral, you may find that your storyline has become dull and lifeless: it will not be as effective as you initially planned.

# The Nuts and Bolts of Creative Writing

## *Brainstorming*

Brainstorming, according to upskillnation.com/brainstorming/, "is a creative process for generating ideas that encourage quantity over quality and discourage criticism and evaluation. A key ingredient for success is allowing thoughts to build on each other." In addition, Merriam-Webster describes brainstorming as "the mulling over of ideas by one or more individuals in an attempt to devise or find a solution to a problem." Usually, brainstorming is an activity best suited to a group situation. I suggest finding a small group of individuals you trust where you can freely share your ideas and build upon them. In your group, you can toss ideas around for future books, merchandise, or any other direction you wish to take as an author or entrepreneur. I have three sisters who have become a sounding board for my ideas and trusted advisors.

Create a brainstorming board using a thinking map with a specific topic or book idea. Members can then throw out ideas written down on the thinking map. Aim to gather as many ideas on the topic as possible. Spend some time discussing these ideas, eliminating any that may not fit. When your groups develop multiple ideas that will work for the topic, build on them. When you are finished, you should have a solid list of ideas that can be expanded upon to create a story that draws readers.

## *Keeping a Journal*

I have been writing for over thirty years, yet I never dared to publish my first book until 2019. I have been writing novels, academic papers, short stories, and novellas since my early twenties, and throughout that time, I have kept notebooks with my stories and journals with my thoughts and ideas. In my experience, this is a practice that you will look back upon and thank the lucky stars you had the foresight to follow at some point in your writing career. I have some journals I wrote and filled up in a couple of months and others where I wrote only a few things every few months, and it took a couple of years to fill up. Either way, I periodically go through them when I am at a loss for ideas. I often don't need them, but I recommend them to all writers, burgeoning or experienced. You never know when your next best-seller idea will come from those pages.

So, what have my notebooks and journals been for me? I love reading and writing, so they have often allowed me to go back and reflect and garner ideas that inspire me to write when all else has failed to get my imaginative juices flowing. I have sometimes found myself reviewing manuscripts I wrote twenty years ago and using my experiences to create fresh ideas within my storyline. I hope to publish all of them one day, but I continue to write, tweak my stories, and dream through my writing for now.

These journals are like my trusted friends. I shared my deepest thoughts and emotions on some of their pages. If anyone were to pick one of them up, they would see that I have bared my heart and soul on many pages, sharing things I have not said aloud to anyone. I have put passion into them that I might not share with even my husband, although I have shared quite a bit with him. They have given me a voice to write what I feel, hear, and see. They have sparked my creativity in ways that might not be true for others. Writing in these notebooks and journals keeps my writing active and is part of my ritual and writing exercise. They help keep my writing and creative muscles busy, mainly when so much is happening around me.

My journals allow me to write freely without judgment, capture my thoughts and feelings on paper, and write whatever I want without criticism or repercussions. Writing with such release is transformational and gets your creative thoughts flowing in ways you may not be able to do otherwise.

Finally, journals are a great way to keep track of your dreams, ideas, and stories you may one day write. They can become beneficial tools used to boost your writing and creativity. They are also an excellent place to practice your writing craft because that is what you want to do.

## *Training Yourself to Describe The World Around You*

When writing stories, we must train our eyes for details in our surroundings. With the hustle and bustle of our busy schedules, we can miss those minute details that will help us develop characters and settings in our stories. These details are what bring our characters and scenes to life. They help us shape who our characters are and develop their personalities. These details cement our setting in our readers' minds, drawing them in so they feel they are in the story themselves. Those details help us tell a story in a way that captures the imagination and makes our readers feel something and become engaged in what we have written.

It's not just the insignificant details we as writers are looking for, but those that provide us with specific and essential information that we would otherwise miss if we were not paying attention. I am taken back to when I was wedding dress shopping with my future daughter-in-law. When looking at dresses, you don't always notice the little things in all the excitement of finding the "one" dream dress. The look in the eyes, the smile on the face, and the glistening of threatening tears tell you all the emotions balled up inside, just waiting to be released. The finer details in each dress, the words exchanged, and the longing and anticipation you can feel.

We must get into the habit of writing down the world around us and paying attention to the small, subtle changes that occur, sometimes seemingly overnight. Things don't usually change overnight and happen over time; we often don't notice the changes until they have transformed enough to pay attention.

As writers, we must learn to pin our writing to specific details to develop good practices. I have said before and will repeat it: read other writers you like or admire. Take your lead from them. Try to keep from using vague or bland adjectives. I recommend keeping a healthy list of adjectives you can use in your writing. The course workbook that comes with this course will provide you with a starting list of adjectives to help you start.

Develop your sensory skills. Learn about smells from perfumes, flowers, and specific odors in the air. Listen for sounds in your surroundings. Learn how to describe different textures and materials to be more descriptive in your stories. Think about various tastes and develop your skills to write about them. Training your eyes to pick up details in your surroundings is learning to articulate your perspective clearly. It takes practice and continually reviewing and editing your work until the details are polished. Get to know what you like and what others want. Write down what each of your favorite foods tastes and feels like in your mouth. Listen to what others have to say about their likes and dislikes. It's all in the details that make the difference in whether your written work is entertaining and engaging or is a dud.

## *Staying Focused*

When I write, I like to be quiet and focused. My husband would be the first to tell anyone that if I am writing, do not disturb me. I get irritable when I am on a roll with writing, and someone comes in or calls me when I am on a mission to finish my train of thought. I know it's not very nice, but I have gotten short with someone for doing that. I must schedule my writing time to avoid this when I know I will not be disturbed. If I believe I will be interrupted, I turn the volume off on my phone, put a note on the door, or let everyone around me know I do not wish to be bothered. Once I lose focus, writer's block will set in, making me frustrated. It is so important to have those quiet moments to write. When that is not possible, I will tune everything around me. I used to work in a warehouse with forklifts going by all the time. With the constant noise and distractions outside my office window, I had to learn to shut things out and focus on the numbers in front of me. You may have to learn to do this if you have not already discovered it. If writing is what you want to do, then make an effort to focus on your craft and let your loved ones and friends know how important it is to you so they will learn to respect your writing time.

## What Do You Like to Write?

Have you asked yourself what topic, subject matter, or genre you wish to write about? One of the things that I find most people have difficulty with is deciding what to write. Getting started is probably the one thing many of my past students have expressed to me as the most challenging. I, too, have had difficulty with this. It is particularly true if I don't have a prompt or a clue about what I want to write. I have found it helpful to get my notebook out and start jotting down some ideas. Sometimes, it is words or phrases; other times, it is little sketches or drawings. I may also write down names I would love to give to my characters. Whatever helps you to gain the traction you need to begin writing, do it! I love writing about things that interest me or that I am passionate about and even things that inspire me. I love mysteries, adventures, historical fiction, romances, and children's literature. I have completed manuscripts in all these areas and more.

Perhaps you have a story you want to share. Write about that in your notebook or on your computer. The best way to know if you will like something is to try it. If you are not naturally adventurous, don't do things that make you uncomfortable. Do what you love and write about it. Writing does not come naturally to everyone, so it will be more challenging for some people. I have had students who hated writing so much they would groan, mumble, and complain every time I told them to take out a piece of paper and pen. I found this to be the case even when I provided them with a topic, a prompt, and the opportunity to do some research to gather ideas together. Don't allow your fears to prevent you from going for your dream. With time, if writing is what you want to do, then with some hard work, effort, and time, you too can become a better writer, embracing all the challenges that come with the job.

## *What Is Your Direction?*

Once you know and understand what you wish to write, you must determine your direction. Are you going to write professionally and make this your livelihood? Will you write in your spare time and publish whenever you can? Perhaps you are like me and start part-time and then move to full-time. Do you want to write articles for journals, newspapers, and magazines? Maybe you want to go full bore and write a novel.

It would help if you decided in time what direction you would take. I am not saying this should happen overnight; I took nearly thirty years to publish my book, as I have mentioned before. I had never published anything in the past, even though I had been writing since I could remember. I had worked with others in writing their manuscripts, articles, and academic papers but could not decide and was too afraid to take a chance on my written works despite being told how good I was. Thinking about your direction will take some thought, but do it; you must.

## *Your Emotional Connection to Your Writing: Real Imagining*

Growing up on an island, I feel connected to that time and often refer back to what I remember. Whenever I can return and visit, I always look for ideas from the scenery, the sounds, the people, the food, and the animals. I believe that writing incorporates our connection to our world, for I never tire of developing ideas from the various sources around me, particularly those that remind me of some experience. I think about the beaches I went to quite often, the sea urchins on the rocks, the small fishes swimming around my legs, the way the waves washed over my feet, the feel of the warm water on my body, or the squishy feel of the sand as I tried to walk through it on my way up the shoreline. I think of my siblings growing up, the friends whose company I enjoyed, or the long, lonely months when my husband deployed with the U.S. Navy.

We are all comprised of our experiences in life, some longer than others, but those shape us and can and often will shape our writing. I lost my dad when I was thirteen years old on Christmas night. To say that I was not profoundly affected by this turn of events would be lying. My dad and I were close despite my parents' divorce, and I felt his loss deeply. It has affected me for a lifetime, and when I write about loss, I think of how his loss made me feel then and how it can still impact me now to share with others that they are not alone in their emotions. Subconsciously, we as writers use our feelings and others to write about their impact on us, even when we think we have moved on in our lives.

When you are developing characters in your story, use your emotional connection to real-life things to give them feelings and help them connect with readers in a real-world way. If I struggle to relate to what my character is going through, I close my eyes and imagine how I would feel and respond to a similar situation. I use my imagination to instill fear, sadness, anger, hurt, happiness, or other emotional responses in my characters. It is much less complicated than we often make it out to be if we put ourselves in our character's shoes.

Remember that your writing is fiction and not autobiographical, even though you use your memories or experiences to create your characters or stories. I embellish for effect and try to detail every scene in a way that makes it realistic or authentic in the minds of my readers. It's okay to tell real stories that are fiction in principle. Using your or someone else's life experiences is okay to tell stories that work, appear genuine, and engage readers.

# Poetry

I am not much into poetry, at least not as I once was, but if poetry is your thing, write it! Do you know of Henry Wadsworth Longfellow, the poet? If not, you should check out some of his work. Perhaps he will inspire you if you are into poetry. There are also many other poets from more modern times, such as Maya Angelou, to consider. Find a poet you can connect with and practice your poetry. It even means emulating their writing and poetic style until you find your writing style. Again, write down your ideas. Get some packets of sticky notepads to jot down ideas for your poems.

Review your high school English Literature classes and think about similes and metaphors you may have learned. Make use of imagery in your surroundings. Sit outside on a chair and watch the sunrise or the sunset. Watch the birds flying by or the little animals in nature scuttling nearby. Think about the smells you sense and the things you hear around you. Use those to help you envision what you wish to write. Sometimes, I smell something that takes me back to my childhood, where I have many memories of the food, the culture, the music, and the people who came and went on the tourist ships that visited our island paradise. When it rains, I imagine the times when I would sit on the porch at my mom's house and watch the water cascading down the pillars. Sometimes, the rains came down in torrents and other times in gentle showers that reminded me of spring. I used to love walking in those rain showers and sticking my tongue out to catch the water. These are keys and clues to help you with your poetry writing. Make good use of the environment around you. You will be surprised by how much you glean from the things around you.

# What is Science Fiction?

While I sometimes watch sci-fi movies, I am not into them. However, I am a *Star Wars* fan and love how George Lucas tells the stories in his films and the creativity and ingenuity of his characters.

What is science fiction, you may ask? Well, it is when a storyteller, whether in books or films, takes readers to a whole new world that, in essence, is an extension of the one in which we all live. The critical factor with a science fiction story is that it diverges with the real world somewhere along the line as we know it and answers the question, what if? Famous stories such as <u>Frankenstein</u> by Mary Shelley and <u>Martian Chronicles</u> by Ray Bradbury answer the question of what if. What if humans could create life? What if we could settle on the red planet? There are many unanswered questions about our world and universe, and our curiosity is unending. People have long wondered about the unknown for quite some time. Writers often use their imagination and creativity to get the human mind thinking about things we often think about but may be too intimidated to ask.

## *Five Tips for Writing a Science Fiction Novel*

Writing a science fiction novel is not for the faint of heart. You should be in it for the long haul because it can be complex. As with any story, you must have a strong plot, create and develop compelling characters, and write a vivid storyline that captures the imagination. Before you begin to write, you must consider five vital things.

1. First, you must have a good idea. Excellent science fiction depends on a great concept that answers implicit or explicit questions. When I think of this fact, I imagine films such as Alien or, as I mentioned, Star Wars, where we could attempt to answer whether there are other beings out there. While these films never really answer the question, they open our imagination to the possibilities and what we might experience if we encounter them.

2. Make sure you are telling a great story. A great idea or storyline is one thing, but can you tell it in a way that captures the imagination, drives interest, and keeps people coming back for more? Is it intriguing, and can it answer whether life exists in other parts of the universe? Can it answer real-world questions people might have?

3. Create an exciting world. Science fiction depends on a writer's ability to create a compelling and exciting world in which their characters live. Does this world interact with our existing one? In what way does it interact, good or bad, and can people relate to it somehow?

Does it reveal your point of view about the natural world in which you live? Your imaginary world should reflect the real world, answer questions, and solve possible problems.

4. As with any storyline, make sure the rules of your imaginary world are consistent. If the story appears choppy or over the place, it will confuse readers or film watchers. It must be logical and maintain that same sense of logic throughout the story. While the reasoning might differ from that in our existing world, it should still be governed by whatever logic exists in that imaginary world. In many Science fiction films and novels, you will see spaceships of all types and varieties. However, how often will you see a movie where aliens come to Earth, are more intelligent, and have technology we may not have seen before? The film *Independence Day*, starring Will Smith, comes to mind. Or perhaps Margaret Atwood's The Handmaid's Tale.

5. Finally, focus on character development. The main characters, supporting characters, and whoever the protagonist and antagonist are essential. Don't allow yourself to only focus on the imaginary world you are creating or the story plot. Developing solid characters with which people can resonate is also the key to a

successful science fiction story that sells. You must establish situations and conflicts for your characters to engage. If you find your characters falling short, develop them more. Go back and review your storyline and plot. Develop them further to see how you can create real emotions for your characters that will impact them emotionally and thus impact your readers or viewers.

# Writing Adventure Stories

When you begin to write an adventure, some characteristics are distinct and help readers identify this type of story. Adventure stories typically take readers from the ordinary to the not-so-ordinary. Your account should hook your readers early on, so they are reading on and on until finally, they reach the end feeling breathless and excited for what you, the author, have next for them to read. Reading a story that immediately takes me into action or grabs my attention from the start makes me a more willing reader.

Before starting to write your adventure story, plan your storyline. Determine who the hero and villain are. Where will your adventure take place or occur? What will your hero do or achieve? What is the villain's role, and how will your hero overcome the challenges placed in their way? How will your story end? Is this a one-time adventure, or will it become a series with the same hero?

As you begin to write, open up your story with a BANG! Use an attention-getter, which may be an action or some dialogue. Perhaps you can use a vivid or detailed description of a particular scene. Whatever you decide, be sure it draws your readers in, grabbing their attention and focus. Use lots of strong and exciting verbs. Use descriptive adjectives to describe sights, sounds, tastes, touch, and smell. When we have twists, turns, and surprises for the readers, they will continue through the story, wondering what will happen next. Mix up the action in as much detail and dialogue as possible. If you drone on and on with words and never break them up, readers could become confused or lose interest. You should also note that the ending is as important as the beginning. Make sure your adventure ends strong and is exciting right to the very end. Take some risks in your writing and create an experience that will remain in readers' minds, keeping them coming back for more of what you offer. Throughout the journey, make sure your hero goes through some metamorphosis. You want your main character or characters to evolve and demonstrate why they are not your ordinary Joe but the extraordinary hero(s) instead.

    Remember the age group you are writing for and ensure your work is age-appropriate. As your readers get older, they will want to see more thrills, and your adventures must be sharp and crisp in detail to continue engaging the same group.

# Tips to Help You Write Your Best Adventure Story Yet

- Read popular novels with an adventure theme
- Structure your story with a basic adventure framework
- Create a compelling main character
- Introduce a catalyst
- Develop strong supporting characters
- Create or find a setting that takes your story to the next level, elevating the risks.
- Pace your story correctly
- Increase the risks your characters take throughout the story
- Set a deadline for your antagonist
- Allow for your protagonist to transform throughout the story

## *Read Popular Novels*

If you are a first-time adventure writer, or perhaps it has been a while since you wrote an adventure, read a few stories by writers you love. Doing this will bring other authors' characteristics, strategies, and ideas to mind. Reading classic adventure stories will help you focus on what you wish to write and how you want your writing to look.

# Structure Your Story With a Basic Adventure Framework

Start with a basic adventure structure, and as you go through writing, put your spin or twist on the formula by creating unique characters, settings, and plots.

## Create a Compelling Main Character

Think about some of your favorite films or television movies. Who are your favorite characters, and why do they stand out in your mind as they do? For me, it is Star Wars. I am a great fan and have watched these films so much that I should own some rights. Ha, yeah, right! I know it will not happen, but I can dream anyway. So, I love Han, Luke, and Leah. I love the sparring between the characters, particularly in the first of the original films, *New Hope.* These characters each have strong personalities and are stars in the movie in their own right. They are unforgettable, and that is what makes them great for the film series.

## Introduce a Catalyst

In the Star Wars film *New Hope*, we see him as a youngster in his late teens, perhaps early twenties, living an average life. When new droids enter his life and stormtroopers kill his aunt and uncle, his life changes as he starts a life-long adventure. Throughout the films, his life and who he is transforms from ordinary to extraordinary.

## *Develop Strong Supporting Characters*

You want to introduce and develop strong supporting characters in your story, as you rarely see a hero accomplishing success alone. Your supporting characters should support the main character's efforts and be engaged in seeking and reaching each milestone throughout your adventure. They are the ones the main character will look to, mainly when the action picks up.

## *Create or Find a Setting That Takes Your Story to the Next Level, Elevating the Risks*

The main character goes from a familiar setting to somewhere unfamiliar or unusual in every adventure. This essential character goes from a typical home setting to a place that is not the norm. This new setting will likely bring out the transformation likely to be seen in the main character and their supporting cast. Some strange twists, a force of nature, supernatural characters encountered, or strange powers in the unique location. The story's landscape now presents challenging situations or creates a dangerous landscape that the characters must navigate.

## Pace Your Story Correctly

My favorite characteristic of an adventure is that it keeps me guessing and constantly in suspense. My hope with my writing is that readers cannot always figure out who the villain is until well into the story or even at the end. I like to keep things moving by creating dramatic plot twists and turns. I review it multiple times to ensure everything moves nicely in my book. I want to ensure readers don't get hung up in any particular area of the story when they go through the book and that it flows smoothly.

## Increase the Risks Your Characters Take Throughout the Story

I find adventure stories that keep the main character asking questions, avoiding danger, and feeling unsettled to be more interesting. It is good to see the main character and supporting team facing challenges and finding ways to work on solutions for the next part. Stacking the odds against the main character throughout their journey fits into an adventure. It would help if you strived for your main character to face multiple risks, including their life, to keep generating interest from readers. You want the climax of your story to be worth the wait and the risks you have taken.

## Set a Deadline For Your Antagonist

Remember, the antagonist usually tries to get away with something they have done wrong in the story. Remember that they will do whatever it takes to maintain their freedom and raise the stakes in every way to reach their goal. Sometimes, it is a race against the clock, like a kidnapping or a ticking time bomb. Other times, it is a journey to beat the protagonist to some goal or location. Whichever you choose for your story, create an antagonist on a quest or mission for something the protagonist wishes to stop them from accomplishing.

## Allow Your Protagonist to Transform Throughout the Story

From the beginning to the end, the protagonist should undergo some transformation. They should change from ordinary to extraordinary in readers' eyes. This transformation may not always be physical but emotional. By providing risks and obstacles for them to endure, you will give them a new perspective or outlook on the world or the people they encounter.

# Writing Suspenseful Thrillers – Tips for Writing Mystery Stories

Mysteries are often intriguing, exciting, and suspenseful, with twists and turns readers may not anticipate. They are not just fun to read but also fun to write. After many years of reading mysteries and watching suspenseful television mysteries, I find these helpful in my journey to becoming a better mystery writer. Try to read mystery novels you love and pay close attention to how the author writes the story. Most likely, throughout, you will see different strategies used to keep the suspense alive and exciting. Look for clues or hints the author drops to determine who the criminal is. Some authors will make it seem like one person for most of the story, only to reveal at the end that it was someone unexpected. If you can, read through the stories you love more than once. You will want to jot down any ideas or clues you read, as they may become helpful later if you write something similar. Remember, as always, to be careful about plagiarizing someone else's work.

When writing about crime, knowing as much about it as possible is essential. Do your research! Remember, the mystery or crime in your story drives it along, so ensure you get every detail as accurate as possible. Know your offense, where it will occur, and when, why, and how. The success of your crime is how realistic and detailed it is. Know your locations for your crime. Research the atmosphere of the crime, study the smells, sights, and sounds, and identify its effects on your senses. Be creative with your descriptions and locations. Find or create a unique space for your crime to occur. I love reading a good mystery and feeling myself in the story. I feel the goosebumps, anticipate the criminal's next move, and travel with the characters as they move from one scene to another throughout the story.

    Open your story with intrigue and mystery right from the get-go. I like opening a good mystery where I am smack in the middle of the actual crime. I love going through the story and learning all the tricks and measures the criminal and the sleuth use to take me on an adventure. I love it when the author drops clues, and I think about who did it. I am intrigued and engaged in the story from start to finish. Imagine my shock when I am completely wrong about who committed the crime.

    Some writers misdirect their readers by creating the belief that one person committed the criminal act, while it turns out to be someone else entirely. When writing a good mystery, it is crucial to show rather than tell. Using descriptive scenes can make your story come alive for readers, allowing them to explore and investigate independently. When I read a good mystery, I always look for clues, examine each potential criminal, and evaluate the crime scene as though I were a detective in the story. I want to solve the crime before the writer gives that information at the end.

Constructing realistic, intriguing, intelligent, crafty, masterful, exciting, and detailed characters is crucial to writing a good mystery. These characters, particularly the main detective and the criminal, should function as the eyes and ears of the readers. They should be relatable and fallible, capable of making the same mistakes the reader could see themselves making. Create a list of potential suspects and have the detective evaluate each throughout the story, eliminating them as you go. I love a good puzzle, which is what writing a good mystery reminds me of when I read it. When I assemble a puzzle, I look for clues to help me. I combine the edges and look for similar pieces to form the middle. When writing a mystery, you will start with essential hints that all the potential suspects will have. As you go through your list, you find differences that help you identify who the actual criminal is. There are always so many false clues in a good mystery that will lead readers down a rabbit hole chasing after the wrong person. This is often done to keep the secret alive and running smoothly.

In the end, you will write, rewrite, and possibly rewrite your story again. I will rewrite it many times before I am satisfied with my plot and storyline. It helps if you reread your story more than once. It is an excellent strategy to follow and will allow you to examine your pacing and redistribute clues to build up to an exciting conclusion. I like to follow through with every detail. I have written notes on my printed manuscript even after I finished. I usually take a break, print it, and then go back and reread it. I make notes in the margin, then go into my computer and make any adjustments. I find it helpful to have a trusted person read the story and give you their feedback before submitting it to your editor.

# How to Write a Romance

Romance novels capture our hearts, and the characters make us feel the intimacy they share and perhaps the intrigue they become involved in within the plot. I love historical fiction, particularly since I love history. Once upon a time, you would not see the intimacy, racy, or steamy scenes now depicted more frequently on television and in films. Love is a complicated subject no matter how you look at it, and it never fails that our emotions or feelings will often get in the way of common sense thinking when we are in love. So, the best thing to do if you want to write a romance novel is to determine what type of romance you want to write and then select your niche. Keep in mind that many romance novels have subgenres, so this can make your story more complicated. Some of these subgenres are as follows:

- Erotic
- Paranormal/supernatural
- Religious or spiritual
- Historical
- Fantasy
- Young adult
- Contemporary

I would not worry too much about whether what you want to write fits into a specific category because it doesn't matter once you decide what type of romance you want to write. I love reading romance novels, especially historical fiction, with a hint of mystery and intrigue. If you're going to write a romance novel, read plenty of them by other authors. I have been reading romance novels since I was a preteen. I read them secretly, unbeknownst to my mother, but I was reading them just the same. My husband likes to call them "B" rated books, just like the ones I like to watch on television. What does he know anyway? To help write your first or next romance, I have a list of tips you can use to help you on your journey.

## *Writing Tips for Romance Novels*

The first tip I already gave to you is to find your niche. The next is to set the stage for your story effectively. What do I mean by this? You want your readers to immerse themselves in your storyline; the setting should invite them to lose themselves in the plot. I will describe historical fiction and some finer points you will see in most of them. They usually occur in England or Colonial America in the 13th through 19th Centuries. There are rules and standards for men and women in England, but mainly for the women in the "Ton." Women have no control over their lives dictated by society's rules, fathers, brothers, or husbands. In some instances, a young lady can find a man willing to be flexible with her interests, which often attracts her to him in the first place. Since society's rules dictate how a young lady should act or behave, any misstep can ruin her future. Also, a woman born into the lower classes of society has potentially no chance of marrying her prince charming in the form of a Duke, Marquess, or Earl. Sometimes, a young lady is fortunate enough to encounter a man from the upper class willing to overlook her shortcomings regarding her birth position. Still, there are often challenges or repercussions that they will face as a result of defying societal rules.

Throughout a romance novel, the characters will often encounter some event or other that causes situations to arise where conflicts may occur. No matter your story, the most critical factor is for the characters to appear realistic and the scenes to be geographically consistent and authentic. Remember that your romance novel is character-driven, so your main couple needs your readers to feel they are head over heels in love. Your "hero" is a man, and the "heroine" is a woman. They can be coupled together as a woman and man or used for a man-to-man relationship or a woman-to-woman relationship; you can apply them however you see fit.

In the typical romance novel, the hero will be dashing, handsome, perhaps wealthy, and muscular. His role is to sweep the heroine off her feet using his good looks and charm to evoke an emotional depth that creates vulnerability in his character, which appeals to the heroine. Don't try to make him a perfect specimen; he should have a past, challenges he has faced or is currently facing, and perhaps he may have even experienced a broken heart. Good heroes should be redeemable and not appear too weak or easy to walk all over. It should not matter where they come from in life. Being a natural rake should not have him permanently dismissed as a bad seed. Whichever direction you choose to take your hero, remember to make him as realistic as possible.

    The heroine should also have experienced some problems. In many instances, she is often in some trouble. It may be her finances, her parents have left her homeless, adopted, and don't know her family history, maybe she is so low down on her luck the hero steps in and makes everything better. The heroine is not a weakling. The heroine should stand alone as a character, and no man, including the hero, should define who she is as a person. She is usually strong in spirit and mind. More often than not, she is feisty in character and willing to stand up for what she believes. She typically displays high courage; she may appear this way despite her inner turmoil as she wrestles with self-consciousness or timid feelings. As she faces her trials, she can gain courage and see her way through to the end. I fall in love with many of the characters in the romance novels I read, and I find them very educational, mainly historical fiction.

Make your characters three-dimensional. Give them realistic flaws and motivations and tie them into their backstory to add a measure of intrigue, mystery, and engagement. You want your readers engaged with your characters from the start of your storyline. Use tried and accurate metaphors or figurative speech to create possible paths for your main couple. Here are some examples of these:

- Friends to lovers- This is a common theme in many romance novels. The main couple grew up as friends in high school or college but have not seen each other romantically.
- Enemies to lovers - It is possible they hate each other at the beginning of the story, and with time, their feelings evolve, and they fall in love. One could be a hardworking middle-class individual, while the other is a spoiled, rich brat who never learned any work ethic. This strategy is often the most effective and realistic in romance novels.
- Healing- in this romance novel, the hero or heroine helps the other with deep psychological problems. Sometimes, this is a broken heart, usually because of unrequited love or perhaps a love interest passed away.

- Meeting again – The central couple has been separated for many years for one reason or another. Perhaps things did not work out between them initially, or circumstances or misunderstandings separated them. Whichever is the case, they ultimately choose each other all over again.
- Mismatched couples – Sometimes, you can have a couple most would not see as likely becoming romantically involved. Do not be afraid to take risks with characters such as these. You can develop your story in such a way that you can add a measure of anticipation or excitement to this couple's relationship.

Regardless of which route you choose, remember that you should put your spin on the storyline, infusing intrigue, suspense, and unique elements that help readers access fresh new ideas.

## *Creating Intimate Scenes*

Your romance novel should have intimate scenes constructed to involve different levels of intimacy and does not necessarily involve sex scenes. There are many romance novels written as clean romances. They are PG-13 and do not involve detailed sex scenes. However, others involve steamy, explicit erotic scenes that are electric and exciting. You will determine how you want to take your story once you decide who your ultimate audience will be. Not all readers of romance novels want to read steamy details, and not every writer can capture such scenes in a way that readers who love these scenes will like. Writing the best intimate scenes will require studying those authors you feel have done well, who you admire, and who will inspire your writing of love scenes. The more you read, the more you will hone your writing skills and create better love scenes readers can enjoy. Your readers will likely tell you if they liked those scenes or not. Use reader feedback to help you give more substance to your settings and to improve your craft.

Also, remember that a sex scene in a romance novel does not randomly happen and is usually there for a reason. Before creating an intimate setting in your book, you should show a connection between your main characters. You want your characters to feel real to those reading your novel. The more realistic your characters appear, the more likely readers will continue reading and return for more of your written work.

One of my pet peeves is when people come up with weird names for sexual organs. Call it what it is, mainly if you are writing erotic romances. It is okay to call them by their scientific name, too. It would be best to consider creating nicknames for body parts in your relationships with your spouse or significant other. I'm just saying.

## *Developing Supporting Characters*

When we begin writing, we forget to create and develop the supporting characters who will take our stories to the next level. As with any genre, build your characters' personalities, dispositions, and descriptions so your readers can connect with them. Your novel should be a well-rounded romance with the heroine seeking out her best friend to share her agonies and triumphs. The hero should have a best buddy with whom he can confide in his confused feelings. No one lives completely alone, so your characters should have people in their lives.

Secondary characters can be best friends, family, neighbors, coworkers, roommates, and an enemy. I have read many romance novels with two competing characters for the affection of the same hero or heroine. All of these characters contribute to the story, bringing it to life. We often fall in love with the secondary characters almost as much as the main ones. They should never be more important than the main characters and should not overshadow them.

## Does Your Romance Novel Have the Potential to Become a Series?

I have seen many authors give a solid secondary character a romance story. Sometimes, an author writes a romance novel intended to stand alone. Yet, because of the strong secondary characters they created, a new story comes to life. As one romantic story reaches its climactic conclusion, another one blooms. There is absolutely nothing wrong with this strategy, and it certainly could help you sell more books.

## *Writing Happy Endings*

While I have never read a romance novel that doesn't have a happy ending, it does not mean I have not read many where a tragedy occurred but did not stop the happy couple from getting together. Those romantic at heart want to see our hero and heroine have a happy outcome to their love story. Many have that "happily ever after" quality, but that does not have to be the case with your writing so long as readers can see a stable couple with a potentially long future ahead of them. Use the ending of your story to tie up loose ends. Perhaps tell about the results of some situation that occurred but does not seem to have resolved itself. It is never good to leave readers hanging unless you plan to expand the main couple's relationship in a follow-up story. Whichever is the case, tie up loose ends by the end of the novel or the series.

## Writing Drama-Filled Stories

One of the things I highly recommend when writing a drama-filled novel is to do your research. I cannot stress this enough, especially if you touch on specific topics, including medical diagnoses or legal problems. You want your writing to seem as realistic as possible, but you will want to have facts to back up your storyline while it may be fiction. Trust me when I say it will be worth the time and effort you put into researching your topics.

Characters in every story are essential, but readers will accept flawed characters more readily when the plot is exciting and keeps the storyline moving along. In a family drama, the protagonists drive the plot, so you must spend as much time developing these characters before you begin writing. Develop your characters so they are strong and can stand up under the pressures they may face throughout your book.

Decide what your crisis or crises will be in your storyline. Determine how the problem(s) will impact your characters ahead of time. Build strong relationships with the characters so they learn to be happy again after encountering whatever problems they face in the story. Identify what the protagonists want and need and look for potential conflicts arising from differing opinions or viewpoints. Significant conflicts sometimes tear a family apart because the people making the decisions may not see eye to eye, although they are working towards the same goal. Eventually, they will have to decide what is more important.

My husband and I will tell anyone who wishes to hear why we have had a long-lasting marriage, accepting that you are not always right. It is okay to admit defeat sometimes; it is better to attain small victories than to go after every big win. Show these types of situations in your story. Put every relationship under a microscope and look at what is going on in their lives. When you write, you become part of the story as you engage with each character on the pages and in your mind. Often, what we see on the surface in a relationship is not always happening behind the scenes. Allow emotions to flow throughout the book. Dig down deep to a level where your words will evoke an emotional response from your readers. Readers will often connect with your characters as they experience their challenges. I cried when reading books because the situation and the words were so relatable; they evoked deep emotions in me, and I felt connected to what was happening with the characters.

I realize we are not therapists but writers; however, it is always good to ask questions about your characters when writing. Here are a few examples:

- Why does a specific character feel the way they do?

- Why does "Jim" have such a bad attitude?
- Why is "Susy" so angry/sad/happy?
- Why/How did this happen to "Cyndi"?
- What can "Bill" do about this situation?

You must fully understand your characters' motivations and determine their meaning. Why? So their actions will be consistent throughout the story. Knowing and understanding your characters' motivations will give your novel more depth and engage your readers at a higher level.

When you think about your life, you can see various stages where a dramatic or traumatic situation impacted you. So, when writing about your characters, consider how you or someone you know might react if they were in a similar case. How would they respond? What would they do? What type of solution might they come up with? Just as you would have much to lose if a significant situation presented itself in your life, so will your characters. Consider throwing in a time limit or consider the emotional consequences of a decision on your characters. Consider logical and illogical solutions to a problem. We all encounter various situations, so use what you know to create realistic conditions for your characters.

## Nailing Your Dialogue

I have mentioned before that you should carry a journal or notebook wherever you go. Well, here we go again! It is always a good idea to get out and be around people. When you have family gatherings, pay attention to conversations. Listen to how people talk or respond in those conversations. Do they interrupt each other? Do they speak to each other? Who or what drives the conversations? When you go back to editing your work, use your notes from these occasions to tighten your dialogue. Eliminate unnecessary words that don't add any value to your writing.

## Use of Metaphors

The use of metaphors in your writing will create atmosphere and suspense. Your use of specific words or phrases using environmental elements will show the tension and feelings of the characters. An event in a cold and dreary winter feels different from one on a bright spring day with flowers blooming in the sunshine. Using nature is a great way to foreshadow events and describe the feelings a character may be experiencing. As writers, we should always seek to hone our craft. We should always be looking for ways to improve our next book. Never give up on yourself, no matter what. Stay focused on your goals, create powerful dramas, and make a statement.

# Writing an Autobiography?

An autobiography is a non-fiction story about a specific person's life, written by the subject from their viewpoint. I love reading autobiographies and biographies about people I like. To be precise, I have read about many well-known political figures, athletes, and movie stars. There is something about learning what brought people to their current place in life and what inspired them.

I will tell you upfront that I have never written an autobiography. With that fact out, here is what I know about autobiographies. Writing an autobiography is a great way to tell your life story and become a keepsake for family and friends. You don't need to be famous or a professional writer to pen your autobiography. Your life story is worth the time and effort you put into it to be informative and exciting. You will want to keep it as factual as possible, especially since many who will be reading it are family and friends. You certainly don't want them questioning the validity of statements you make in your book. Unfortunately, many of us do not believe our lives are meaningful enough or would be suitable for such a small audience. You can print at least fifty copies and sell them or give them to those you desire to have a copy. Any one of us is capable of writing our memoir.

One of these days, perhaps I will write my autobiography, but I have not decided. Like many of you, I don't think my life merits an autobiography, but what do I know? Don't let that stop you, though. Here are some tips to help you on your journey:

1. If you are going to write an autobiography, get to work reading other autobiographies to see how they were written. Billy Graham and Maya Angelou are two individuals who wrote autobiographies. You can also search the internet to find other autobiographies, and I am sure you will find someone who has written one that appeals to you. It is good to read different writing styles to help you better understand how to write your autobiography.

2. Understanding your intended (target) audience will determine your next steps. When you write for a general audience, the tone and choices of words will vary. You will not use the same word choices and tone when writing a keepsake autobiography that your children, grandchildren, and future generations will enjoy. For example, when describing familiar settings and people, you may not use as many details as you would in a general storyline. You may share anecdotes, interesting facts, and events that perhaps family members may not know. Of course, it is okay to

add specific details to an event. You will also include your perspective and memories of particular events when writing your autobiography. Suppose you plan to share your autobiography with individuals outside the family. They may not be familiar with some or all of the events you write about in your book. In that case, it is always good to err on the side of caution and include specific details. Doing this will help people outside your family understand your story better.

3. Develop your core concept for your autobiography. Perhaps you have encountered hardships throughout your life and have found success. You experienced different challenges, learned some valuable lessons, and want to impart wisdom about the lessons you have learned on your life journey. You never know when what you write about will inspire others.

4. Think about all the different periods of your life. Make notes about specific events as you recall them. Long-forgotten events might come back to you only as you sit and reflect. As your memory returns, write down everything that comes to mind. You may find that recalling these events has new meaning or that you can piece together different events to show how you have grown through challenges. I have boxes of family photos, and when I go through them, I can always

come up with memories from when we took those photographs. I have kept letters, greeting cards, and various things my children and husband gave me throughout the years—all of these you can use to stir up memories and help you write your autobiography.

5. Before you begin to write, you should organize your story. Decide where you will start, what you want to say, and how you will say it. If I were to write an autobiography, I would likely write it chronologically, from birth to where I am now. Another option would be to arrange your book according to your life's significant events or themes. Whichever way you choose to format your life story, it will help if you keep everything organized. Don't forget to include photographs or information that will help document events.

6. As with any other written work, find time to write as often as possible. I try to make this a daily habit, but sometimes life gets in the way. You will need that quiet time and space to focus on what you wish to write. I write during the day as my husband is at work and my children are grown, so I have few interruptions. Some people like to write with quiet music in the background, but I like total silence to clear my mind and focus.

7. No one wants to read boring words. Do not take this personally; I am not saying your writing will be boring.

I suggest that each of us needs to keep our writing exciting no matter what we write. When I reread my work, I check to ensure that my writing flows smoothly, that there are no confusing areas, and that my details are accurate but not overwhelming. I ensure each paragraph transitions well, as I don't want my readers to get bogged down or stuck on a particular word or phrase. If I am reading and trip up, my readers will, too. You will also want to remove unnecessary words and phrases when editing.

8. Writing tools are essential to keeping your writing accurate and looking polished. I highly recommend a program such as Grammarly or some other software to check for grammar, spelling, and sentence structure accuracy. Also, if you struggle, do not hesitate to use an online autobiography template to help you get started. There is no shame in seeking help. You will find there are many options on the internet to assist you.

9. Edit, Edit, Edit is what I am going to say here. Editing and improving your work is a process that will pose challenges, but every writer, whether burgeoning or professional, has to go through this. I have mentioned this before. Consider someone you can trust to read through your finished work. They may spot mistakes

and provide suggestions for changes. Ultimately, you will have the final say about what goes into your autobiography, so remember, you do not have to make any changes other than those necessary to correct writing errors. If you are reviewing your work, take a step back and come back later to read through it again. I usually go through my work multiple times, and more often than not, I find errors or make changes because something needs to sound right or feel wrong.

# Point of View

What is a point of view in writing, and why is it so important? As a fiction writer, a point of view is the imaginary world you enter when writing. Your choice of point of view is essential since it determines your story's tone while affecting characterization and plot. Usually, this will be in the first or third person. For example, in this course, I write primarily from the first-person point of view as I give my perspective and reference experiences or knowledge on specific topics. From a third-person perspective, it would be, "They walked together through the park gazing at their surroundings in wonder." For most writing assignments, avoiding the first- or second-person and writing from a third-person perspective is best. If you choose to have your narrator in a story, speak from a first-person perspective. Be careful not to allow your voice to become that of the narrator, or they will take on a color of their own, and the lines will become blurred as a "shadow author" creeps into your novel. Overshadowing can create doubt and cast a shadow over your whole book.

Your readers trust you to stay on point, and they may only stick with you for a short time when you break that trust. Refrain from wavering in your writing or point of view. Avoid taking such risks and use dialogue and conflict to add different voices by these means. Remember to ask yourself the question, whose story is it anyway? Choose wisely the point of view you will use and determine ahead of time what strategies you will engage in to ensure you will stay on the path. Is it your story?

# Plot, Structure, and Narratives

This next section will briefly discuss plot and structure, but not in extensive detail, as I have a separate course that addresses these two topics.

## What is the Plot, Anyway?

The plot is what happens in a story. I know some of you will want to plan out every detail of what you wish to write before you begin, but I am not one of those writers. I will make notes and have a basic story premise, but I rarely have every detail accounted for initially. Once I sit down to write, I just let the words flow from my mind to paper or computer until I run dry. Sometimes, the entire story comes out simultaneously; other times, it comes in various stages. I often go back after each chapter and read through my writing. I will also write ten chapters and then take a break to review where I am in my story. Regardless of how you write your story, in the end, you will have a plot in your completed manuscript.

When I write, I don't wonder whether my plot will work. If I sat there all day long worrying about whether my plot would work, I would not get any work finished. After finishing my novel, I want to know the plot is clearly defined. You want to connect with your readers, which is vital to success. When readers, agents, or publishers pick up your novel, they ask questions. They may ask about the story and why they should read it. Some may be bold as to why they should care. As a writer, you must be prepared to answer these questions and know how your plot will benefit others. Is there anything happening, and will it engage me? There are other questions they may ask, so be aware of this and put yourself in a position to ask them truthfully and accurately. Creating great characters is essential, but what happens in your story is more important.

## *Structure: The Glue That Holds It All Together*

The structure is what pulls your story together. Timing is everything, and in your written work, it should matter. Structure assembles all the various parts of your story, making it accessible to readers. You want your story to be organized and manageable so it can be transparent to readers. The plot represents the elements that will go in a story, while the structure determines where the writer places those elements within the story. Writing a solid plot and structurally pulling your story together is something other than what a writer should do halfway. Think strongly about how your plot will affect the outcome of your book and how you will structurally bring it together to capture and engage your readers.

## *Narratives*

When you seek to create grand narratives for your novel, you must understand your target audience and what they expect when they pick up a book to read. Find some potential candidates who may become customers and create a focus group. Ask them questions beforehand and then follow up by having them read your finished piece to obtain critical feedback. These responses may surprise you, allowing you to review and refine your work to reflect what your readers wish to see. Readers often want to be captivated and entertained, have thought-provoking responses to the written word, and be entranced. I want to feel as though I have become a part of the tale as an innocent onlooker. I will have this same feeling sometimes when I am actively dreaming. It is like being there and seeing and hearing everything but not being able to do or say anything to change it. Other times, I am engaged in the dream and speaking, but it seems surreal. Active narrative structure gives the story the strength it needs. Consider how your central nervous system works in your body. The central nervous system functions as a processing center for the nervous system. Its job is to receive and send information to the peripheral nervous system. Our brains process and interpret the data. So essentially, the book's narrative structure is the book's spine that upholds the characters and holds descriptive passages together. The narrative should show tension and emotions and withstand the test of time as reader after reader goes through it, sometimes even rereading it. Ultimately, the narrative you choose for your novel will significantly depend on what you write and what words will be required to take your writing to the next level.

# Making Tough Decisions

Making tough decisions is more about knowing and understanding the world around you and determining how and what role it will play in your story. You have to know what the world acts, feels, and sounds like so you know what it will feel and sound like in your written work. If you create an imaginary world in your book, it is vital to understand your world first, mainly if your characters from both worlds interact. You must create movement between the two worlds and know how to make that happen realistically for readers. In our world, we do things a specific way, and if they are going to be different in the new world you create, you have to determine the impact on your characters when they transition from one world to the other. Suppose a specific behavior is allowed in one world but not another. In that case, you must create ways for your characters to adapt to the cultural differences or develop conflicts in the story to reflect the differing rules. The decision will be up to you, the writer, to decide how best to address these issues.

## *Reaching the Finish Line?*

Have you finished writing, or have you? That is the crucial question. Once you finish writing your manuscript, you should consider taking a step back. If you have a deadline in mind, this does not mean waiting for months to review and revise. It likely means perhaps days, but no more than a few weeks. When you return, you may have a new perspective and look at your written work with fresh eyes and ears. As I have said, have someone you trust to read your work and make suggestions, perhaps even put notations in the margins. While reflecting, these suggestions or ideas help refine your work as you read through your writing. While writing my initial manuscript, I constantly wrote and revised words and phrases. Yet, even after I have written everything I can think of, I always find myself coming back and finding things I could change to improve my work. There is nothing wrong with that! You must read what you have written and do so repeatedly to ensure it says and will have the impact you desire.

Reading through your work is not just so you can assess and polish your words, but you can dig deep between the lines and address structural issues for cohesion. Again, here is a great time to apply the software to manage problems by looking at sentence structure, comprehensive grammar, and spelling. The formulation of everything is just as important as what you have said. I think of it when I am cooking a meal. When I cook, I throw different ingredients into the mix to create a delicious and delightful feast for the tastebuds. Most great chefs refrain from throwing random things into their meals. They have a plan, they have specific ingredients, and they follow a recipe to the letter. This same principle applies to any great novel. As a writer, you don't put random words in the story, or it would be one big jumbled mess. No, you create a plot, develop characters, decide on the correct narrative, mix it all, and then return to check that everything works.

## *Revising: Making Necessary Changes*

When you are writing anything, it becomes part of a process that can sometimes prove difficult right to the end. Even after you finish, you must revisit your work to adjust. After completing your reading, you must make the required changes you have noted and then read through your work again. Yes, I know that sounds tedious, and depending on your writing, it may be so; however, nothing good will come of sitting back and relaxing before your written words are groomed and polished to a shiny brass finish. Like a photographer seeking to weed out those photos that do not meet minimum requirements, does your writing meet with wordsmithing strategies that have some of your words falling by the wayside only to be replaced by other words? Through this process, you refine your work so that what readers hold in their hands is the very best of who you are as a writer. This process is an essential step you cannot avoid, as redrafting is always needed. Go the extra mile when you write a book. It is not for you alone. Once the readers get their hands on it, the writer and the reader's imagination collaborate. We often write in quiet and solitude, but once our books are released, they become public. As you write in private, you are working on ensuring you bring the best of your writing and imagination to readers. Once you publish, whether you have accomplished this becomes the readers' decision. Ultimately, you want your readers' imaginations to expand and experience what they desire from your written work.

# Your Book is Finished: What Now?

## *Outside Reviews*

Once your finished manuscript is edited, proofread, and prepared to your satisfaction, it is time to publish your book. After publishing it, you will want professional reviewers to assess your book and provide you with a review. Depending on the reviewer, this could take weeks or months. You can search online and find professionals to review your book. Once you find a few, contact them to inquire about their requirements, fees, etc. No, they do not do it for free. You can probably solicit free reviews from other reliable sources, but be aware of who you choose.

## *Listening to Constructive Criticism*

When you offer criticism to someone else, it is not the same as being on the receiving end. Remember that only some people who give words of criticism are correct in their assessment of your work. If constructive criticism is constructive, it will be valuable and help you adjust your writing. Unfortunately, some people will be mean regardless of how good their work is and will have something negative to say no matter what. Do not allow the words of those individuals to get into your headspace. When criticism is well-founded, it becomes valuable to you as a writer and is used for educational purposes to improve your skills. It is essential not to take constructive criticism personally. Be confident and recognize that criticism doesn't mean you cannot write or are a horrible person. We often define ourselves by the criticism we receive, but we must learn to separate the two when writing. You are not defined by what you do for a living. Genuine constructive criticism should foster a desire to experiment with and grow your writing skills, taking you to the next level in your professional writing career. Once you receive that constructive criticism, make adjustments, let it go, and move forward. Refrain from getting caught up in other people's opinions of you. After all, their opinion should not dictate how you live and what you wish to write about moving forward. Their opinion should only seek to enhance your written work positively.

## *A Dynamic Finish: The Final Run*

When you write a book, there are some things to consider when all is said and done. First, you should plan. I thought I had planned everything out, only to discover I was not even close. By this point, you have considered your content, proofed it, and are ready to print and publish it for all to see and read. However, did you consider marketing, your target market, the costs associated with marketing, and who or how you will proceed? I was so excited about getting my book in the hands of readers that I did not seriously consider the time this would take, the money it would cost, and the methods I would use to sell every copy. I was sidetracked when I received several proposals to market my company and books. Not that their pricing wasn't fair, but I had not considered or budgeted for them, and my bank account was screaming. It would help if you thought of all the costs before you begin the process to avoid the disappointments I have felt in my inability to proceed as I desired. If you are like me and are self-publishing a physical book, there are costs you should plan for:

- The publisher's fees
- Graphic layout and design (they will not be included in the publisher's fees)
- Illustrations/licensing fees (if needed)
- Editor fees
- Proofreading fees
- ISBN, barcode, and copyright fees
- Printing
- Marketing/advertising costs
- Initial and ongoing website costs
- Professional reviews
- Writing associations (not a requirement)

- Travel expenses to promote your book

I am sure there are more than just these; however, these immediately come to mind as of this writing. I hope you will make a list during the book's planning stages and ask questions to ensure you are emotionally and fiscally prepared to embrace your new venture.

## Agents: Should you get one, and why?

To get an agent or not. That is a question many of us have asked before venturing forward with writing our book. That was an easy one; I needed an agent or, in my case, a Brand Stylist with the skills and knowledge to help me publish my book. Her advice and services have been invaluable to me, and I have no regrets about utilizing her services. This decision is a personal one and will require some thought. My publisher came highly recommended to me through a mutual friend who had her book published through the same company. Do your research and ensure that whoever you choose has a known track record for seeing things through. It is crucial as you want to avoid finding yourself halfway through your project left high and dry. Ask questions if you are self-publishing; you should have some control over your work, the pricing, the illustrations, the layout, and everything that happens with your book. Be aware of hidden costs associated with publishing your book through certain agencies. I am not trying to knock any particular agency to ensure that prices do not blindside you or find out later that you will only receive 8% - 10% of earnings from your book sales. Read everything carefully! An agent will help you weed through the fine print and guide you through the process. They will conduct the follow-ups, get the word out about your book, and help you decide where to submit your book or who to contact for a chance to review your manuscript. An agent is not required! I know of several individuals who published a book using software on the market for creating eBooks. I initially wanted to start with a physical book, so I have just attempted to work with eBooks.

There are many changes in the marketplace for writers—literary agents, literary consultants, brand stylists, publishers, printing presses, and printer publishers. However, you look at them; the list is long, and the fees vary. Professional advice is essential and sometimes necessary for many reasons. Whether you contract with an agent for the long haul or contract for specific services, think long and hard before deciding. Good luck!

## On to the follow-up

Remember that everything you put out about your book requires constant follow-up. Either you will be completing this task, or you will have to hire someone to complete it. The crux of the matter is that you must constantly put your book in front of readers to continue successfully making sales. It is the nature of sales, and it requires commitment and dedication. Plan and prepare for how this will look for you.

## Reading Critics

Finally, ignore the haters. No matter how well you write, you will always find those people with something negative to say. Constructive criticism is okay but watch out for those mean individuals who want to make you feel just as miserable as they are. Being genuine in your stories is OK, but remember that not everyone wants to be authentic.

# Conclusion

As you conclude this course, use the following workbook as a tool to help you fine-tune your skills and knowledge. I wrote this course to help you learn some tips and tricks when writing. Creativity is within each of us, and we must reach deep and pull it out, kicking and screaming. Not everyone will immediately recognize or acknowledge their creativity but don't give up on yourself or your dream of becoming a great writer. You are more blessed than you realize, and with some guidance, knowledge, and perhaps a little kick in the seat of the pants (not literally), you can attain your desires. If all else fails, please contact me on my website: https://www.magrasliterary.com.

I offer one-on-one personalized services for those seeking further assistance with their writing. I also provide other writing courses designed for you to work at your own pace in the comfort of your home. Thank you for trusting me with your creative writing needs. I look forward to hearing from you.

**Susan M. Edwards, Authorpreneur, Speaker**

# References

www.upskillnation.com

de Bono, Edward. 1986. **The Six Thinking Hats**

Lucas, George. 1977. Star Wars film *New Hope*. (Originally Released by Lucasfilm now a part of the Disney Family)

# OTHER BOOKS BY THIS AUTHOR

**STORIES**
- CUPCAKE ISLAND: THE KIDNAPPED PRINCE (2024 REVISION COMING SOON)
- THE HIBISCUS CLUB MYSTERIES: THE MISSING NOTEBOOK (COMING SOON IN 2025)
- MAKING FAST FOOD: A CARIBBEAN-BASED CHILDREN'S STORY (COMING SOON IN 2025)
- ENCHANTED SNAKE ISLAND: THE MISSING TIARA (COMING SOON IN 2025)
- JOURNEY FROM DEPRESSION TO FREEDOM

**COOKBOOKS**
- CARIBBEAN MEDLEY: A COMPILATION OF CARIBBEAN-AMERICAN RECIPES
- DESSERTS AND BREAD (COMING SOON IN 2025)

**INFORMATIONAL BOOKS**
- THE COMPLETE RESUME GUIDE: LANDING THAT COVETED JOB
- CREATIVE WRITING COURSE WORKBOOK

**PUZZLE BOOKS:**
- KID'S CHRISTMAS ACTIVITY BOOK
- KID'S THANKSGIVING PUZZLE BOOK
- KID'S HALLOWEEN PUZZLE BOOK
- CHRISTMAS WORD SEARCH
- BIBLE-THEMED WORD SEARCH

- HALLOWEEN PUZZLE BOOK
- THANKSGIVING PUZZLE BOOK
- VALENTINE'S PUZZLE BOOK
- MUSIC AND INSTRUMENTS PUZZLE BOOK
- FOODS, FOODS, FOODS PUZZLE BOOK
- DOGS AND CATS PUZZLE BOOK
- FOURTH OF JULY AND SUMMER PUZZLE BOOK
- SEASONS PUZZLE BOOK
- SPORTS PUZZLE BOOK

## FOLLOW US ON:

- **FACEBOOK:**
    - MAGRAS LITERARY ENTERTAINMENT
    - THE HIBISCUS CLUB MYSTERIES
    - THE TRAVELER'S DETECTIVE AGENCY BOOKS
- **INSTAGRAM:**
    - MAGRASLITERARY
    - HIBISCUSCLUBMYSTERIES
    - TRAVELERSDETECTIVEAGENCYBOOKS
- **Amazon:**
    - Susan M. Magras-Edwards

## WRITING SERVICES:

Visit us at www.magrasliterary.com for your writing needs. You can also email us at magrasliterary@gmail.com or connect with us via our website. Please email us to receive our monthly newsletter filled with updates.

www.ingramcontent.com/pod-product-compliance
Lightning Source LLC
LaVergne TN
LVHW051848080426
835512LV00018B/3144